THE CASTLES OF
PENDENNIS
AND
ST MAWES

RICHARD LINZEY, RIBA

Introduction

Facing each other across the sheltered waters of the Fal estuary, the castles of Pendennis and St Mawes are witnesses to over 450 years of history. Standing on the crest of the Pendennis headland, or by the sea at St Mawes, you can appreciate the strategic significance of this part of south Cornwall. Falmouth was the first or last port of call for many ships before the vast expanses of the Atlantic, while its calm waters provided a safe refuge from storms.

This 'Key to Cornwall' had to be defended against attack by enemies, whether by land or sea, to prevent it being used as a 'stepping stone' to invasion of this island. The defences themselves reflect 500 years of changing technology in warfare, from early cannon to the nuclear age. They have also seen action, during the Civil War of the seventeenth century, and the two world wars of the twentieth century. For over 300 years the Pendennis Headland was the objective of Spanish and French invasion fleets. During the twentieth century the castles were fortified to defend Falmouth against German attack. Falmouth was also an embarkation point for the D-Day allied invasion fleet that changed the course of the Second World War.

The castles also have a story to tell about the men and women who built, lived and worked in them. They reflect the power of kings and queens, but also the lives of ordinary soldiers and their families through the ages, in war and in peace, and the local communities of which the castles are part. Today Pendennis and St Mawes stand as links with our past. Pendennis shows us how things have changed through time, while St Mawes looks much as it did when built in Henry VIII's time. We hope this souvenir guidebook, its tours and history, helps bring this fascinating story alive.

CORNWALL'S GREATEST FORTRESS... FIVE CENTURIES OF DEFENDING BRITAIN'S COASTS

NATIONAL EVENTS

1538–41 Fear of invasion from France and Spain, then war with France

1588 Spanish Armada

1596 Spanish fleet heading for Fal estuary blown back by gales

1642–49 English Civil War

1652–54
1665–67 } Wars with Dutch Republic
1672–74

1689–97 War with France

1701–13
1738–48 } Wars with France and Spain
1754–63
1776–82

1779 Spanish and French invasion fleet plans to seize Falmouth

1789–1815 Revolutionary and Napoleonic wars with France

1847
1853 } Invasion 'panics'
1859

1914–18 First World War

1939–45 Second World War

1952 Britain tests own nuclear bomb

1956 Coast batteries dismantled

1500

1600

1700

1800

1900

2000

PENDENNIS AND ST MAWES

1540–45 Henry VIII orders building of the castles

1598–1600 Pendennis fortified with ramparts and bastions

1627 More land defences added to Pendennis

1646 St Mawes surrenders to Parliamentarian army without firing a shot. Siege of Pendennis: Royalists defend castle for five months. Queen Henrietta Maria and the future Charles II escape the country from Pendennis

1715 Report on poor condition of both castles

1730 Pendennis Headland defences strengthened

1793 New gun batteries built at Pendennis and St Anthony. New stores built at both castles

1848 More powerful guns at Pendennis

1880s Electric minefield in the estuary channel

1890s New gun batteries built

1901 New barracks built at Pendennis

1939 Pendennis and St Anthony become main harbour defence, commanding south Cornish coastline

1944 Guns last fired in action

1956 Pendennis and St Mawes decommissioned and troops leave

PENDENNIS CASTLE
Description and Tour

First, visit the Discovery Centre. Then, walk back to the centre of the parade ground and across to the entrance of the round tower in front of you. Use the bird's-eye view of the castle below, and the colour-coded labels to guide you around the site.

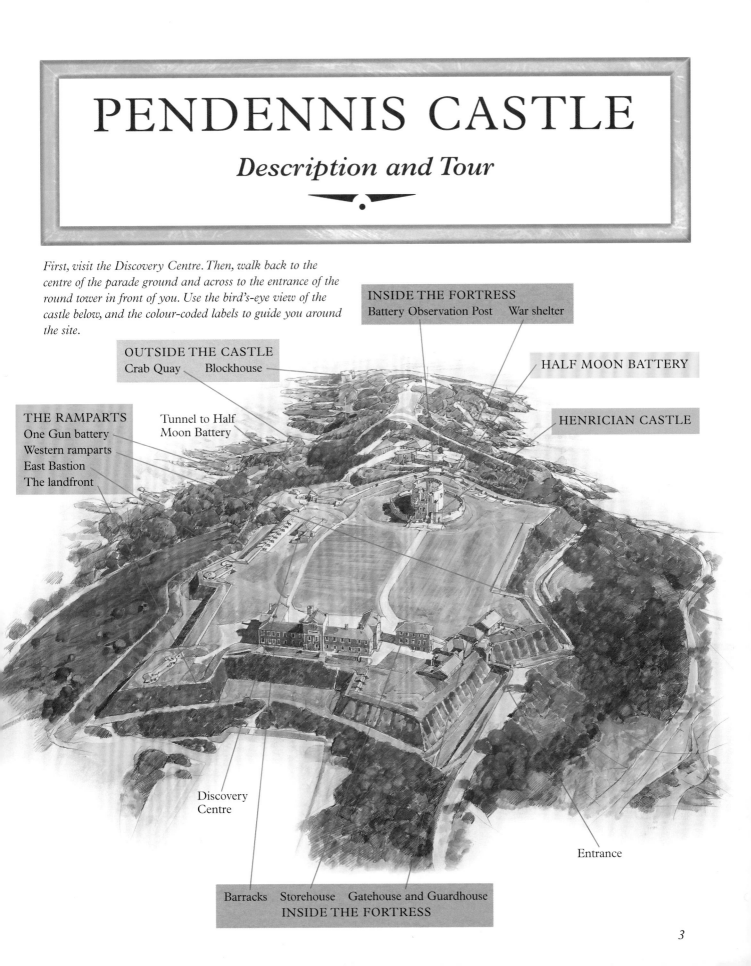

INSIDE THE FORTRESS
Battery Observation Post   War shelter

HALF MOON BATTERY

HENRICIAN CASTLE

OUTSIDE THE CASTLE
Crab Quay   Blockhouse

THE RAMPARTS
One Gun battery
Western ramparts
East Bastion
The landfront

Tunnel to Half
Moon Battery

Discovery
Centre

Entrance

Barracks   Storehouse   Gatehouse and Guardhouse
INSIDE THE FORTRESS

THE HENRICIAN CASTLE

Henrician castle

This is the most westerly of the chain of artillery forts built under Henry VIII's orders between 1540 and 1545. It consists of three distinct parts: a central round gun tower, an encircling low circular gun platform, and a projecting entrance block or forebuilding overlooking the parade ground.

The central round tower is the oldest part, but its lower gun room was superceded almost immediately by the multi-sided 'chemise' or external gun platform that surrounds the tower. The present forebuilding, with its imposing bay window, was added in the second half of the sixteenth century, replacing an earlier forebuilding.

The building was probably last armed during the Civil War, after which time it was used for accommodation and storage. The open floors were partitioned up into small rooms, and the first floor was used as a residence by the castle's governor and his lieutenant. In the mid-nineteenth century, it became an armoury and storehouse, and briefly served as an officers' mess before being passed to the Ministry of Works in 1921. It was reoccupied during the Second World War and once more served as the officers' mess and headquarters for the Falmouth Fortress Commander.

The castle is well built, of granite from Polrudden, near St Austell, with the rougher stone coming from the Mabe quarries to the west of Falmouth.

BELOW *The Henrician castle, with the forebuilding facing you. The arch and wall are all that remains of the Tudor guardhouse*

Entrance

You enter the castle through an arch in a ruined wall. This is all that remains of the single-storey Tudor guardhouse, built as part of the original design. This was demolished at the end of the nineteenth century and replaced in 1902 by a mock-Tudor building which served as the headquarters for the local militia. This itself was demolished in 1923.

The stone bridge also dates from 1902, and replaces an earlier wooden drawbridge that spanned the dry rock-cut ditch. Above the entrance door is a fine carving of the Tudor royal coat-of-arms. Below this is an empty recess, probably where the governor of the day could display his own coat-of-arms. The two columns either side of the main door originally supported a beam over which the chains connected to the drawbridge passed before entering the loopholes behind to connect to the portcullis. This ingenious counterbalancing mechanism overcame the need for cumbersome winding gear inside.

Turn left inside the door. This room may have been intended as a guardroom. During the eighteenth century it was used as a 'parlour', or private living room. Notice the eighteenth-century cast-iron grate displaying the three cannons of the Board of Ordnance. This was the body in charge of forts and cannon and responsible for appointing the governor. To the right of this room is another area with a large fireplace and baking oven that may have acted as a kitchen for the governor's lodging, even though it was also the main route into the building and up the spiral staircase to the other floors.

In front of you is a doorway and a small lobby. This was once the main entrance before the forebuilding was built. Note the defensive gun loop added to defend this entrance.

Basement kitchen

From the small lobby, go down the spiral staircase into the basement.

The basement contains a cooking hearth and ovens. The area would have originally been subdivided to serve a variety of purposes, including kitchen, cellar and larder. At one time there may have been a well here, to provide fresh water in times of siege. There is also a latrine.

Ground floor gun room

Return up the spiral stairs and turn right into the ground floor gun room.

This octagonal room has gunports (called 'embrasures') in seven of its sides. The openings through which the cannon fired were originally circular, but have been adapted to fit square windows.

Looking through them you can see it would have been impossible to fire through these once the 'chemise' had been built. It is possible that this gun room could have been used if the threatened invasion by Spain and France in the early 1540s had materialised during the construction of the tower. The room served as a mess room and barracks for the garrison. The gunners would have slept in hammocks or on the floor, and eaten their meals here, brought up from the kitchen in the basement below.

Upper gun room

This floor now houses a reconstruction of a Tudor gun room. The cannon are replicas of the type of cannon known to have been at Pendennis in the sixteenth century. There would have been a wide mix of weapons: some cannon were modern models cast in

ABOVE *The upper gun room, with reconstructions of Tudor cannon and equipment*

ABOVE *One of the grotesque waterspouts decorating the forebuilding. The details are all finely carved*

ABOVE *The wooden portcullis*

BELOW *The governor's dining room, furnished with modern 'craft' pieces in the spirit of the eighteenth century*

bronze, others old-fashioned wrought-iron breech-loaders mounted on wooden slides. One of these guns can be seen in the display. Henry VIII's castles were always lacking equipment because the Crown lacked the money to arm them fully.

Each gun recess, or 'casemate', contained a gunport with a wooden shutter that could be raised and lowered as necessary. The sockets you can see were for a beam to hold the shutter closed. Ropes and pulleys enabled the guns to be pulled back to the firing position after they had recoiled on being fired.

Discipline was essential for working in such a confined space. Despite the Tudor builders' efforts to ventilate each casemate, the conditions in this room when the cannon were fired must have been similar to those on board a warship of the time: cramped, noisy, dark and choking. The gunpowder would have given off a thick acrid smoke that would have lingered in the room.

The roof

Climb up the spiral staircase to the roof.

The most important gun platform would have been on the roof. A boarded floor was built above the leaded roof to bear the weight of the cannon. The lookout turret is thought to have been the location from which the great Spanish Armada of 1588 was first spotted from the mainland. It has its own small fireplace.

From here you can enjoy the best views across to St Mawes on the other side of the estuary, and westwards past the estuary of the Helford River towards the Lizard.

To reach the roof of the forebuilding, go down the steps through the parapet to the north.

The Governor's Lodging

From the roof of the forebuilding climb down the wider spiral stairs in the turret to the first floor.

You are now on the first floor of the forebuilding. In Tudor times, these rooms may have been used by the captain (or governor) of the castle, although we have no evidence for their use. For most of this period, the captains were members of the Killigrew family, who lived only half a mile (1 km) away at Arwenack. By the early eighteenth century, when the duties of governor had become more ceremonial than functional, the rooms formed part of the governor's lodging, as did the former gun room, which was partitioned up into five bedrooms.

The three rooms now contain modern furniture and fittings to give a sense of scale and use. The first room has eighteenth-century panelling. The portrait is of Philip Melville, who held the governorship during the Napoleonic period and was well-known both for his strict discipline and for his humanity towards his men.

The second room was the finest, lit by the bay window. It is furnished as if it were a bedroom. There is a latrine and closet in the far corner. It is possible that the window could have doubled as a gunport in times of war. The third room, above the entrance, contains the portcullis.

INSIDE THE FORTRESS

Storehouse
Barracks
Gatehouse
and Guardhouse

The large expanse of open ground in the interior of the castle was not always like this. From the early days of the fortress there had been a succession of houses, barrack blocks, stores and general buildings inside the ramparts to serve the garrison. Many were temporary structures, often made of wood, that have disappeared without trace. For example, during the Civil War, the area was occupied by a windmill, houses and gardens. During the First World War there was a hutted camp, and during Second World War the area was covered by prefabricated corrugated-iron Nissan huts.

Gatehouse and Guardhouse

The earthen ramparts you can see today were built in 1598–1600, during the reign of Elizabeth I. The earliest entrance to this fortress consisted of a counter-balanced drawbridge, with an arched passage through the rampart and a freestanding arch on the other side of the ditch. This arrangement was replaced by the present gatehouse and guardrooms in the late seventeenth century. The guardrooms are possibly the earliest purpose-built barracks in Britain.

The room above the gate was used as living quarters by the Barrack Sergeant in the nineteenth century. In the mid-nineteenth century, the lower floor of the northern block was converted into two detention cells and a guardroom. A small exercise yard for prisoners and a rifle and ammunition store for the guards were added in the early twentieth century. The southern block, now the ticket office, was used for stores and as a bootmakers' shop.

The guardhouse and cells have now been restored to give a suggestion of their appearance during the First World War and provide a flavour of garrison life at the time. Army rules were strict, and petty offences, such as drunkenness or neglect of duties, could result in soldiers spending time locked up in these cells.

BELOW *The gateway, built around 1700. The remains of the Elizabethan entrance can still be seen within the main arch. The fixed bridge is modern, but incorporates the stone piers of an earlier wooden drawbridge*

ABOVE *The guard detention room, furnished as it may have appeared during the First World War*

ABOVE *From left to right; the sergeants' mess, guardhouse, storehouse and Royal Artillery Barracks.*

Storehouse

The storehouse, now housing the shop on the ground floor, was built during the Napoleonic wars, sometime between 1793 and 1811. Used to house both artillery stores and the everyday necessities for the garrison, it was later converted into a hospital and then, in the early years of the twentieth century, into a canteen for the soldiers.

Royal Artillery Barracks

The barrack block was completed in 1902 to house the 105th company of the regular regiment of Royal Garrison Artillery, consisting of about 140 men, that arrived at Pendennis at the end of that year. The block was divided up into rooms for 11 or 12 men, with the corporals and sergeants having their own rooms.

Discovery Centre (field train shed)

The building now housing the Discovery Centre was built during the Napoleonic Wars to store a 'field train' – a horse-drawn detachment of artillery stored at the fort that could be sent to trouble spots when needed.

War shelter

The earth mound to the south of the Henrician castle covers the remains of a gunpowder store (or 'magazine'), probably built in 1733. Around 1895 the magazine was radically altered to create a war shelter for the gunners manning One Gun Battery. It has now been restored to how it may have appeared at that time, when it would have been used by the gunners to sleep and eat in during times of emergency.

· CANNON AND GUNS ·

In Tudor times there were many names for cannon, including culverin, falcon and saker (named after snakes or birds of prey), although using these names did not necessarily denote a set size of bore or length. Later cannon and guns were standardised by either the width of their barrels (e.g. 6-inch), or the weight of the shot they fired (e.g. 12-pounder). Early cannon fired solid stone or iron shot (cannon balls). Later innovations included chain shot (smaller balls connected by a chain), grape shot (small balls), and canister shot (a shell filled with small musket balls) that would inflict greater casualties on attackers at close range. Later guns fired shells filled with high explosive. Rifled barrels, with grooves inside the barrel, gave the shells more spin and made them travel further with greater accuracy.

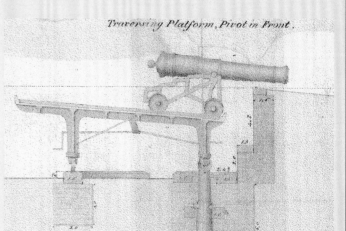

An early nineteenth-century cannon, from a drawing of proposed changes to Half Moon Battery

Battery Observation Post

During the nineteenth century, Half Moon Battery became the main offensive gun position at Pendennis.

When the battery was reconstructed in the late nineteenth century, an observation post was built on the ramparts to control the battery. From there, observers could use a position finder to judge the distance and position of a target and relay that information by telephone to the gunners in the battery below. The gunners could then adjust the guns so that the shells would hit their target.

The present Battery Observation Post was built during the Second World War to co-ordinate the fire of the two 6-inch guns then installed in Half Moon Battery, and its related searchlights. From this room, observers could monitor shipping movements in the English Channel and receive reports from other coastal observation and radar posts between Portloe in the east and St Agnes in the west.

The instrument on the table allowed an observer to translate a ship's position at sea directly into measurements of latitude and longitude and then, via mechanical data

LEFT *The interior of the reconstructed war shelter. The order 'stand to' has interrupted a meal!*

processors, into accurate gun settings. These were then transmitted to the guns of Half Moon Battery by Magslip transmission – an early form of remote control.

This room has now been restored to its wartime appearance. The walls are painted dark blue as originally to reduce reflected light. Above the window is a panorama of the coastline that could be used as a quick reference chart by the observers.

BELOW *Members of a re-enactment group in Second World War uniforms inside the Battery Observation Post. Following an enemy vessel through the position finder telescope accurately plotted its position on the map table below.*

THE RAMPARTS

From the centre of the parade ground, go to the East Bastion, halfway along the rampart overlooking the Fal, and then follow the ramparts of the fortress clockwise.

Henry VIII's forts had been designed to counter attack from the sea, and were vulnerable to a land siege. In the late sixteenth century, the castle was surrounded by ramparts and bastions (see box opposite) to protect the castle against attack from the land, increase the number of guns and protect storehouses and barracks.

The ramparts would have presented a formidable series of obstacles to any attacker. Before the mid-nineteenth century, the slopes were kept free of trees and bushes, so the defenders on the ramparts would have had a clear view of an approaching enemy force. The counterscarp – the slope on the far side of the ditch – was made as steep as possible. The ditch was always dry – but any attackers who reached this far and who tried to scale the walls, or undermine the rampart, would have been subject to cannon and small-arms fire from the flanking bastions on either side, with no place to hide.

East Bastion

East Bastion was modified in the late nineteenth century to create two emplacements for quick-firing 12-pounder guns to defend the channel into the harbour against fast-moving torpedo boats. Ammunition stores (magazine) and a war shelter for the gun crew were cut into the solid rock beneath. The ventilators helped keep the volatile explosive in the store at the correct humidity and temperature.

During the Second World War the magazine was converted into a plotting room for all the fixed gun batteries at Falmouth. Further along is a battery of nine cannons of late eighteenth- and early nineteenth-century

date, commanding the harbour channel. The battery dates to major improvements made to Pendennis in the 1730s by Colonel Christian Lilly, the engineer in charge of the West Country's defences.

One Gun Battery

In the late nineteenth century, the bastion at the south-east corner of the fort was virtually destroyed to make way for a new reinforced concrete gun emplacement, known as One Gun Battery. This was built to hold a 6-inch 'disappearing gun'. Three of these guns were fitted at Pendennis, one here and two in the remodelled Half Moon Battery (see page 12).

The disappearing guns used hydro-pneumatic technology (water, glycerine and air in a piston mechanism) to lift the heavy barrel above the parapet. The recoil after firing would bring the gun back down to its original position for reloading, out of the line of return of fire. The idea was that the 'disappearing' action made the guns more difficult to spot and protected the gun crew.

The guns were never proved in action and were also prone to mechanical breakdowns. Furthermore, it became evident that a rolling ship at extreme distance would have difficulty in hitting a shore battery and the disappearing mechanism fell from favour. The gun in One Gun Battery was eventually removed in 1913. During the Second World War, a battery of 12-pounder guns was placed on the ground near the dismantled One Gun Battery.

BELOW LEFT *A carronade, named after the Carron factory in Falkirk, Scotland, which produced these effective short-range weapons*

BELOW RIGHT *One Gun Battery, with the view across the channel to St Mawes in the background*

cavalier

fraize

salient

bastion

ditch

counterscarp

The weaknesses of Henry VIII's forts lay in the 'dead ground' created in front of a round tower where a defender could not see an attacker. By the later sixteenth century the use of earthen-backed walls or ramparts with projecting angular bastions had become standard to overcome this defect.

The slope of the ramparts absorbed the impact of cannon balls, while the projecting bastions allowed smaller guns to provide covering fire if any attackers tried to scale the ramparts. A wide ditch gave defenders a clear field of fire from the main armament mounted on the ramparts. Sometimes a raised gun platform called a 'cavalier' was added to a bastion to give the defenders extra height over their attackers.

The gun currently displayed in the emplacement is a 6-inch breech-loader, on a test mounting that allows it to be displayed at the same height as a disappearing gun.

By the side of the magazine for One Gun Battery is a tunnel cut through the rampart. This was originally the site of the Elizabethan postern, or sally port, from which defenders could reach the defences outside the ramparts. At the end of the nineteenth century it was remodelled, and a further rock-cut passage made in the counterscarp, to give access to the Half Moon Battery.

The southern rampart

At the far end of the fortress is the Battery Observation Post for the Half Moon Battery (described on page 9). The large grass mound covers a war shelter. Nearby, to the right, are emplacements for more guns, with one Victorian muzzle-loading shell gun mounted on a reproduction traversing carriage. This allowed the gun to be moved (or traversed) along the section of rail using block and tackle. These guns were probably used for practice.

Western ramparts

At the south-west corner of the fortress is Pig's Pound Bastion. Here there is a nineteenth-century carronade, a small cannon used for firing at any attackers in the moat trying to approach the rampart. You can see another carronade facing it on Horse Pool Bastion opposite.

The land front

At the north end of the fort, behind the barrack block, the ramparts were improved during the Napoleonic Wars with elevated gun platforms, called 'cavaliers', added to protect the landward side. Cannon mounted on these would have been able to direct fire down onto any attackers approaching the ramparts. The ditch is wider here than elsewhere and the two bastions on either side would have provided intense cross-fire.

Smithwick Bastion, on the side nearest the entrance, contains the castle's last magazine, completed in 1898. Carrick Mount Bastion, on the other side, has emplacements for two quick-firing 12-pounder guns installed in 1903.

BELOW *Tunnel cut through the ramparts leading to the Half Moon Battery*

HALF MOON BATTERY

Half Moon

*W*alk back to One Gun Battery and go through the tunnel on your right. This leads through the ramparts to the Half Moon Battery.

The principal offensive firepower of Pendennis first moved away from the shoreline and the fort on Pendennis Point in 1793 when a new battery was built below the ramparts. This was in the shape of a half moon, thus giving the battery its name. It pointed towards the mouth of Falmouth Harbour, concentrating the offensive firepower of the castle out to sea.

The original battery was for cannon, but in 1895 it was completely reconstructed to mount two of the three 6-inch breech-loading 'disappearing guns' (see page 10). These were replaced by more conventional guns in 1911. Emergency work carried out after the declaration of war against Germany in September 1939 remodelled the battery and made it Falmouth's principal line of defence.

The battery today has been reconstructed so it appears much as it did at the end of the

ABOVE *Inside the underground stores of Half Moon Battery. Notice the special lamp in the glass-fronted alcove. Shells and cartridges are shown here side-by-side, but in reality they were kept strictly separate.*

Second World War. The late nineteenth- and early twentieth-century underground magazine and war shelter can be visited with a guide.

The battery is armed with two 6-inch naval guns similar to those mounted here during the war. Guns of this type had a range of up to 12 miles (18km). The concrete canopies you can see were built

over the gun positions in December 1940 to protect them from the new threat of aerial attack. Camouflage netting would have hung from the canopies to disguise them from the air. The hooks for the regulation gas masks, helmets and capes that the gunners had to have with them on duty survive on the wall.

During the Second World War, the gun commander would have received information on the range and bearing of targets direct to the guns by electric signal from the Battery Observation Post on the ramparts above (see page 9). Corrections for speed, wind direction and tide were made via the plotting room in the East Bastion.

The greatest threat came at night, when detection and accurate firing were more difficult. Searchlights on Pendennis Point could therefore be co-ordinated to illuminate possible targets for the guns.

In 1944, the detachment needed to staff Half Moon Battery and its associated searchlights and communications 24 hours a day totalled 99 men and women. Of these, the gunners made up only 36, with most of the remainder operating the searchlights or involved in the position finding and communication tasks, showing how important these jobs had become in modern warfare.

⩗ LOADING THE GUNS ⩘

The underground stores as they appear today are arranged symmetrically – each half is subdivided into separate shell and cartridge stores for each gun. The shells themselves were filled with high explosive. The cartridges contained the charge to propel them. This was originally gunpowder, but by the late nineteenth century had mostly been replaced by cordite, a smokeless explosive.

Loading the guns, c.1911 (sketches by Ivan Lapper)
RIGHT *Passing the cartridges through a hatch to the hoist*
BELOW *Handling the explosive shells*

ABOVE *Carrying the shells to the hoist which lifted them to the gun emplacement*
LEFT *Once cartridge, shell and fuse had been loaded into the gun it could be fired*

The explosives were volatile, and every effort was made to keep them apart until they were loaded in the gun. Precautions were also taken to prevent sparks igniting them. Soldiers working in the magazine had to wear special clothing and canvas shoes. They changed into these in the 'shifting lobby' at the entrance to the cartridge store.

The lamps used to light the underground rooms were protected behind thick glass. A special room, called the lamp room, was used to maintain the candle lamps used underground. By the Second World War the magazines had been equipped with electricity, making the lamp room redundant. Alterations in 1940 made the shell and cartridge hoists redundant and ammunition was thereafter carried up to the guns by hand.

LEFT *Looking along the barrel of one of the 6-inch guns towards St Anthony Head where an answering battery of two 6-inch guns was situated*

OUTSIDE THE CASTLE

Crab Quay
Blockhouse

Many of the defences of Pendennis Headland lie outside the castle ramparts. A separate leaflet provides a selection of walks around the headland with full details of what can be seen today, but the main features are described below.

Crab Quay Battery

The shoreline by Crab Quay is the best landing place on the headland, and as early as 1700 was controlled by a guardhouse. A battery to the north of it mounted cannon closer to sea level than the ramparts of the castle. The guardhouse was later converted to a machine-gun post, but you can still see the loopholes for muskets in the wall.

What you see today dates from the late nineteenth-century when the battery was armed with two 6-pounder quick-fire guns (note the concrete emplacements). Behind the gun positions are the shell store of 1902 and a small cartridge magazine dating from 1851, itself later converted to a shell store. A passage linked the battery to the guardhouse. The guns were removed in 1906, but the battery was briefly reoccupied in 1939–40 when two 3-pounder quick-fire guns were installed. The concrete bases that you can see at the waterline are all that remains of the emplacements built for searchlights supporting Middle Point minefield battery to the north.

Peter Gilson

LEFT *Looking from Pendennis Point towards Crab Quay Battery, with the concrete emplacements for the two 6-pounder quick-fire guns installed in the early twentieth century clearly visible. Together with a matching battery at St Mawes, these guns would have provided powerful crossfire against any torpedo boats trying to sink shipping in the Carrick Roads*

The Blockhouse (Little Dennis)

This defence was almost certainly built in 1538 as a stop-gap measure to mount a number of cannon until the main castle could be completed. There were originally several gun positions, but these were soon replaced by a single gun firing through a larger gun port similar in style to those in the castle above. It would have fired at any enemy ship sailing into the Carrick Roads and the safe anchorage of the Fal estuary.

Blockhouse Long Platform and Lower Fort

During the reign of Elizabeth I, the blockhouse was incorporated into a fort encompassing the whole of Pendennis Point, with three batteries at sea level, a ditch and drawbridge. This almost certainly adapted and strengthened existing Henrician defences.

The fort itself fell out of favour in the eighteenth century, but the main battery, known as the Blockhouse Long Platform, was retained until superceded by Half Moon Battery. This platform mounted cannon to protect the harbour mouth. Traces of the walling for this battery can be seen in eroded sections of the cliffs.

Above the blockhouse, the levelled area marks the site of the unfinished Point Battery, dating from the late 1840s. Parts of the rock-cut ditch can still be seen. On the shoreline are the bases of searchlights used to illuminate targets for Half Moon Battery.

Middle Point Battery

The patch of dense scrub behind the picnic area at Middle Point marks the site of Middle Point Battery, constructed during the Second World War for twin 6-pounder quick-fire guns. A multi-storey concrete 'director' tower was built behind the battery, from where targets could be observed, searchlights directed and target information passed to the guns. All the surface features of the battery were demolished in the 1960s.

ABOVE *The blockhouse, the earliest Tudor fortification on the Headland*

ST ANTHONY HEAD BATTERY

An aerial photograph of St Anthony's Battery, taken during the Second World War, shortly after it was hit by an enemy parachute mine in 1941

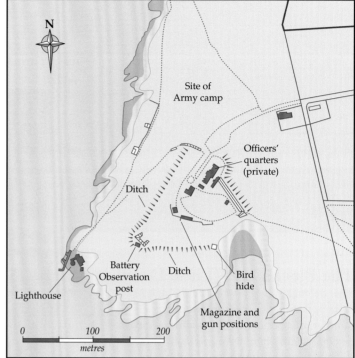

The view from the ramparts of Pendennis Castle is one of the finest in south Cornwall. If you look out across the water you will clearly see St Anthony Head, with its distinctive white lighthouse. Closer to the open sea than St Mawes, by the late eighteenth century the headland had became the preferred site for a battery to defend the entrance to Falmouth Harbour, in combination with the defences of Pendennis.

A half-moon-shaped battery of four 24-pounder cannon was created on the headland in 1796, but after the end of the Napoleonic wars it was demolished by the local landowner, Admiral Spry. In 1895–97, a new battery was built to mount two 6-inch guns. The battery was manned by regular troops until 1911, when it reverted to territorial units. The guns were removed at the end of the First World War, but the battery was kept in serviceable condition, and was rearmed soon after the outbreak of the Second World War. They remained part of the frontline of Falmouth's defences until the end of the war when the battery was put into 'care and maintenance'. It was decommissioned in 1956, and in 1959 the site was acquired by The National Trust.

What can be seen today are some of the buildings associated with the battery – the range-finder posts, guardroom and officers' barracks (now used as holiday cottages), and the site of the gun emplacements. The magazine, which is among the finest surviving in this country and retains its original shell and cartridge hoists, can be seen by prior arrangement with the National Trust. More temporary structures, including Nissan huts, were demolished in the 1950s.

As the battery was remote from the other fortifications, the whole area was surrounded by a deep rock-cut ditch with spiked steel fencing and protected by a bastion at its southern end containing two machine-gun nests. In 1939, a new observation post was built in the ditch in front of the battery. This has been repaired and can be visited.

From the fort you can walk down to the lighthouse, built in 1834.

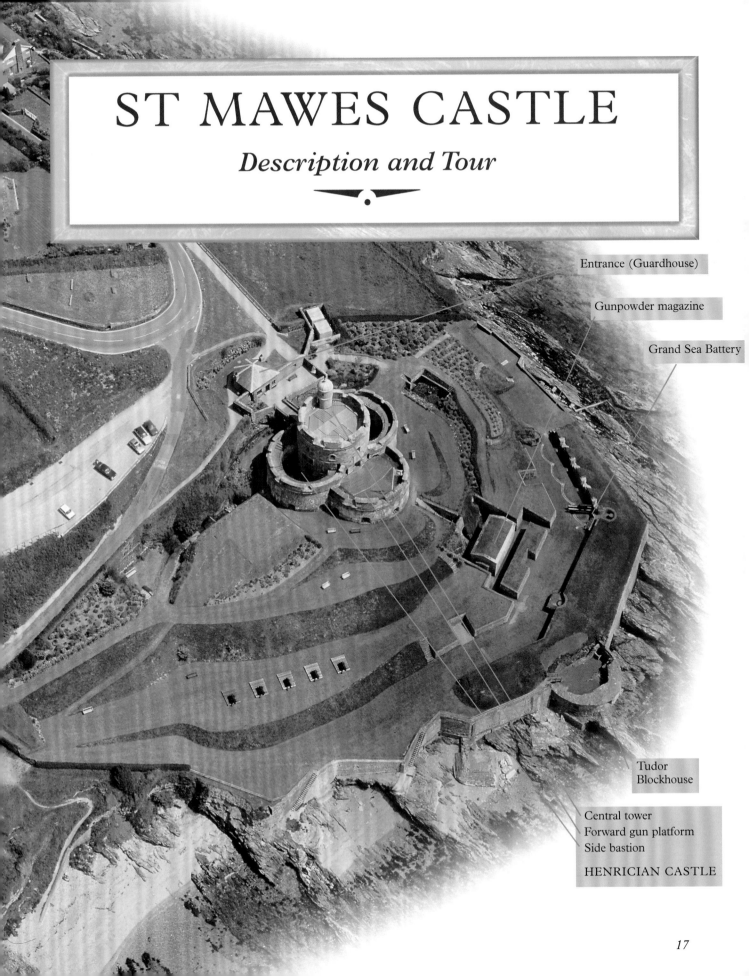

ST MAWES CASTLE

Description and Tour

Entrance (Guardhouse)

Gunpowder magazine

Grand Sea Battery

Tudor Blockhouse

Central tower
Forward gun platform
Side bastion

HENRICIAN CASTLE

ST MAWES CASTLE

St Mawes Castle is a unique combination of Tudor technological prowess and a celebration of the power of the monarch. It is a purpose-built artillery fort, yet great care was lavished on the quality of the masonry and the details of gun loops, windows and heraldic carvings. The ditch would originally have encircled the entire castle, but was largely infilled when the outer defences were improved during the reign of Elizabeth I.

The castle comprises a circular central tower with three lower bastions, or 'lunettes', arranged on the seaward faces like the leaves of a clover. The main entrance is on the landward side, protected by a rock-cut ditch.

Guardhouse (entrance)

The ticket office occupies the outer lodge or guardroom. This was originally octagonal, but was cut back in the eighteenth century when the yard behind it was roofed over to form stables for the castle.

A stone bridge spans the ditch. Over the main door is a fine carving of the Tudor royal coat of arms. Above this is the first of a series of carved inscriptions composed for the castle by the king's antiquary, John Leland, when he was a guest of Thomas Treffry during the castle's construction. These verses praise Henry, and his son Prince Edward (later Edward VI), who as heir to the throne also held the title of Duke of Cornwall. The Latin inscription above the door reads:

SEMPER HONOS HENRICE TUUS
LAUDESQUE MANEBUNT

Henry, thy honour and praises
will remain forever.

Inside the castle

Cross the bridge and enter through the doorway. Once in the corridor turn right.

The entrance door leads into the second floor of the central tower. There is one floor above this, and two below, all connected by a spiral staircase. Immediately on the right is a glass panel in the floor. This covers a deep shaft down to a small punishment cell known as an 'oubliette'.

The area inside is divided into three rooms by original Tudor partitions: two smaller ones on either side of the central corridor with a larger room at the far end. Each of the small rooms has its own fireplace, and the left-hand one has a window to light the main stairs linking the floors.

At the end of the corridor is a door frame, elaborately carved with the heads of two figures and inscriptions on scrolls saying 'God save King Henry VIII' and 'God save Prince Edward'. This door leads to a large room running across the width of the building. The room has a fireplace, with a recess above it, probably for the royal or the governor's coat of arms. There are two openings either side of it. One was probably used for storing salt (salt was often kept near a fire to keep it dry) while the other could have been used for warming plates or re-heating food brought up from the basement kitchen. This floor, with its fine decoration and private rooms, was probably the private quarters for the captain or his lieutenant.

Forward gun platform

At the far end of the large room, through the doorway with the series of arches above, and down four steps, is the forward gun platform or west bastion.

Four cannon would have been sited here, firing through the gun ports or 'embrasures'. From here you can see that the position has a good command of the Black Rock channel and the safe anchorage between St Mawes and the Pendennis Headland. You can see the Black Rock in the sea between St Mawes and Pendennis.

If you look back above the door there is more ornamentation, with a carved panel in low relief of King Henry's coat-of-arms, most of which is worn away, but originally may have been painted. On either side are two figures, perhaps 'tritons' or sea gods, holding scrolls with more of Leland's verses.

SEMPER VIVET ANIMA REGIS
HENRICI OCTAVI QUI ANNO 34 SUI
REGNI HOC FECIT FIERI

May the spirit of King Henry VIII, who had this castle built in the 34th year of his reign, live forever.

Wall-walks

From the platform take the right-hand door as you face the central tower.

This leads to the wall-walk around one of the side bastions. Just inside the door you can see a latrine in the inner wall. The slots in the stonework are for fitting a wooden seat.

The embrasures in the wall-walk wall are for hand-guns. In each you can see the hole in the centre to support the swivel-pin of the gun and at the top of the parapet the sockets for a wooden shutter that could be raised or lowered as necessary. The recesses in the wall held supplies of shot.

Upper gun room

Re-enter the main tower and go up the stairs to the next floor.

The top internal floor was a combined gun and barrack room but, like the side bastions, it was designed for hand-guns only. We know from the lists of weapons in Henry's castles that all the castles were well provided for in terms of bows and arrows, and early muskets (or arquebusses), as well as short-range breech-loading cannon such as the one on display. From this room the garrison could defend the castle from an infantry assault. Each of the medieval-style windows has a vent to allow gunsmoke to disperse.

The stairs lead up to the roof, and then on up to the turret. In Tudor times, the roof was used as a gun platform. The turret was used as a look-out point.

ABOVE *The forward gun room. The cannon on the right is the bronze saker retrieved off the coast near Teignmouth*

BELOW *Detail of the decoration and royal coat-of-arms above the door from the tower to the forward gun platform*

drawbridge. There may have been a well in this room originally, as under the castle there is a virtual lake of fresh water from streams that drain into the sea. In times of emergency, the kitchen would have to supply regular meals not only to the regular garrison but also the local men who had mustered to defend the castle.

Mess Room

Go up the stairs to the floor above the kitchen.

The floor above the kitchen was probably the garrison's mess room. This was the main living area for the regular gunners for most of the castle's life. Like the other floors of the castle, the area was formally partitioned up into smaller rooms. During the late nineteenth century the castle was used as married quarters for the gunners.

The largest room on this floor had a fireplace. In one corner are a small fireplace and cupboard that may possibly have originally been used by the castle armourer as space to carry out weapon repairs and bullet-moulding.

BELOW *The fireplace in the basement kitchen*

Kitchen

Go down the stairs to the bottom floor.

In the basement of the tower is the kitchen. Like the other floors it was originally subdivided. The larger room contains a fireplace, with a brick-lined bread-oven built into it. The granite pedestal table, by the entrance, may have been for a jug and beakers of drinking water drawn from the drip well which can be seen beneath the

---

· ARTILLERY FORTS ·

Henry VIII's artillery forts were revolutionary in England in their time. They were specially designed to mount cannons and resist bombardment. The round gun towers and semi-circular bastions were used as gun platforms. Enemy cannon balls would be deflected off the curved surfaces and immensely thick walls, while the squat profile provided a difficult target for an enemy firing from onboard a rolling ship.

Reconstruction drawing by Alan Sorrell of St Mawes

Forward gun room

Climb down a flight of stairs to the lower floor of the forward bastion.

This, and the platform above, was where the main offensive armament of the castle was situated. Each alcove, or 'casemate', has a smoke vent and sockets for a beam that would have held a wooden shutter. Most of the guns on display are ships' cannon from about 1800, but in the centre is an impressive bronze saker of about 1560 cast by the famous Venetian gunmaster Alberghetti. This was recovered from the sea off Teignmouth in Devon. This is just the sort of gun with which the castle was first armed. Documents reveal that the castle had three of these bronze sakers.

Side bastions

Facing the stairs you came down, walk towards the arched passage to your right.

Once through the passageway, two small rooms appear. These were the garrison latrines and probably discharged into the sea. You are now below the wall-walk you passed along earlier. Here there are three more casemates for heavy guns.

Retrace your steps, go across the gun platform and through the passage on the far side.

You are now in the north bastion. Here again there are three casemates for heavy guns. In the centre is a water pump installed in 1849, together with the reservoir beneath your feet.

BELOW *View of the central tower and lookout turret*

THE SHORE BATTERY

ABOVE *One of the blank shields on the bastions*

To enter the gardens go back to the main entrance and turn right after crossing the bridge. Go through the arch and down the steps.

From the outside of the castle you can see that each bastion has a blank shield with a further quotation from Leland's verses. That on the south bastion reads:

GAUDEAT EDWARDO NUNC DUCE CORNUBIA FELIX

Rejoice Happy Cornwall now that Edward is Duke;

that on the west reads:

HONORA HENRICUM OCTAVUM ANGLIE FRANCIE ET HIBERNIE REGUM EXCELLENTISSUM

Honour Henry VIII, most excellent king of England, France and Ireland;

while that on the north side reads

EDWARDUS FAMA REFERAT FACTISQUE PARENTUM

May Edward resemble his father in fame and deeds.

Follow the path and down the steps to the large gun by the sea wall.

Grand Sea Battery

As at Pendennis, the favoured position for mounting guns at St Mawes became not Henry VIII's artillery fort, but the shoreline in front of it. During the Napoleonic Wars this area was remodelled to form what became known as the 'Grand Sea Battery', with up to twelve cannon. The castle was used for accommodation for the gunners.

As at Pendennis, the guns in this battery were updated several times to meet changing needs and developing technology. In the mid-nineteenth century the battery was remodelled to mount 12 'shell guns'. At the end of the century, these were replaced by four 64-pounder rifled muzzle-loading guns on traversing carriages. You can see the rails for some of these carriages, and a reproduction of one of them with a 12-pounder cannon. By 1890 these in turn had been replaced by two 5-inch breech-loading guns, used in conjunction with a new minefield.

To the right of the gun you can see the concrete plinth for a quick-fire 6-pounder gun, also introduced in the late nineteenth century. This too was replaced by a pair of 6-pounders of which one platform remains further to the right. These seem to have been a stop-gap measure because they were later removed and a battery of four 12-pounder quick-fire guns placed in the field above the castle, with a better command and field of fire, together with its own underground stores and defence works.

Gunpowder magazine

With your back to the sea, walk down the narrow passageway between the walls in front of you.

This building and the steep stairs behind it were built in 1854 to serve the new battery of shell-firing guns on the improved battery below. The magazine was divided into two unequal spaces, the larger of which held the cartridges for the explosive shells fired by the guns. The smaller room was originally fitted with shelving to store the shells themselves. The walls have ventilation slits to help maintain a level temperature and humidity inside. Timber lining throughout helped reduce the danger of sparks igniting the powder. Soil and turf on the roof helped reduce the impact of a direct hit.

The Tudor blockhouse

Make your way back to the sea wall and then turn right until the wall ends. Then turn sharp left along the narrow path by the railings and down the steps.

Just as the blockhouse built on the

BELOW *The earth-covered magazine of the Grand Sea Battery.*

LEFT *The Grand Sea Battery, with the Henrician castle in the background and the magazine of 1854 to the left*

shoreline below Pendennis Headland provided offensive firepower (see page 15), so a matching blockhouse was built at St Mawes. Like its twin, it was built before the main castle. Slightly larger than the blockhouse on Pendennis Point, it had three gun-ports, and there is evidence of a small fireplace and oven, and a water cistern. Originally it would have been roofed, with guns mounted on the roof itself, but was reduced in height during the nineteenth century to form part of the sea-level battery.

On the shoreline are the remains of concrete emplacements for searchlights, once camouflaged to look like the rocky foreshore. These were built at the beginning of the Second World War to provide illumination for the newly built quick-fire gun battery at St Mawes.

Leave the blockhouse and walk up to the lawn terrace on your left.

Here are five cannon dating from the reign of George III (1760–1820). You can see his cypher of 'GR' and the figure 3 intertwined on the barrels.

Underneath the entrance bridge you can see the spring-fed drip well cut into the rock on your left. Reclimbing the steps will bring you back to the entrance lodge and exit.

• QUICK-FIRE GUNS •

Reconstruction drawing by Colin Fearon of one of the 6-pounder quick-fire guns installed at Crab Quay Battery in 1904 (left) and a naval quick-fire gun in use (right)

By the 1870s, military strategists were worried about the threat from steam-powered torpedo boats that could move faster than the large coast defence guns could aim, fire and reload. Gun manufacturers responded by developing 'quick-fire' guns that could fire shells at rates of up to 12 rounds per minute and provided a better chance of hitting a fast-moving target.

KING HENRY'S CASTLES

ABOVE *King Henry VIII, in a portrait by Hans Holbein from 1537, just one year before work started on the blockhouses at Pendennis and St Mawes*

ABOVE RIGHT *The Tudor royal coat-of-arms, from above the entrance to St Mawes Castle*

The west of Cornwall in the early sixteenth century was a long way from the centre of power. Contemporaries viewed it as the 'ends of the earth'. In 1506, a ship carrying Philip of Burgundy sought shelter in what is now Falmouth Haven. The Venetian Ambassador to Castile who was on board wrote:

We are in a very wild place which no human being ever visits … in the midst of a most barbarous race, so different in language and custom from the Londoners and the rest of England that they are as unintelligible to these last as to the Venetians.

This isolation, and the survival of its own language and customs, combined with a rugged conservative individualism, made the county very different from other areas of England. Cornwall was however neither poor nor under-developed. Thriving tin-mining, fishing and coastal trading made towns such as Fowey, Truro, Penryn and Penzance prosperous. Local gentry families often had more influence over local affairs than representatives of the king, and traditional rights and ways of doing things were jealously guarded.

The sheltered waters of the harbour were a popular safe haven from storms for ships in the English Channel, and were used for ship repair and as an anchorage by the early Royal Navy. They were also undefended, a shortcoming that was highlighted in January 1537 when a Spanish fleet attacked a group of French warships in the estuary and forced the French ships aground off Truro. A local gentleman, John Arundell of Trerice, intervened, arrested the participants and made them disperse, but issued a request to London that:

We desire the King's help to have blockhouses made upon our haven, else we shall have more of this business.

The king's plans

In 1538, the balance of power in Europe shifted against King Henry VIII of England. Since his divorce from Katherine of Aragon in 1530 and his break with the Pope over control of the Church in England Henry's position in Europe had become difficult. England was one of the smaller countries of Europe and much of Henry's diplomacy was targeted towards maintaining a balance between England and its neighbours. In 1538, his two main European rivals, Francis I of France and the Emperor Charles V, made a treaty in which they also agreed to help the Pope reclaim England for the Catholic Church.

The king began to organise musters of men, hire mercenaries and prepare the coastline for an attempted invasion. Part of these activities was to improve the defences of ports, possible landing sites and anchorages and fortify them where necessary with strategically placed artillery blockhouses to deter ships. The Fal estuary was selected as the site of two of these forts.

Blockhouses mounted with cannon, flanking an estuary, had been introduced at many southern and western ports in the late fifteenth and early sixteenth centuries. Often a chain connected to floating barrels was stretched between the two blockhouses in times of trouble. It was probably during the preparations of 1538 that two blockhouses were built to guard the Fal at St Mawes and at Pendennis Point (Little Dennis) as interim measures until the new castles could be built.

Building the castles

Work on the castles proper started in April 1540 for St Mawes and October 1540 for Pendennis. Both castles cost over £5,000 each (a large sum of money at that time), although the precise building accounts have been lost. Both took about five years to complete, although some of this time may have been spent on the outer defences at Pendennis after the two castles were operational.

Sir Thomas Treffry, a local landowner, who had built a blockhouse at Fowey, volunteered to supervise the building of St Mawes. Here the castle consisted of a central circular keep with three semi-circular bastions, or 'lunettes', all mounted with cannon. Michael Vyvyan of Trellowarren was appointed the first captain, or governor, of the castle, with Treffry as deputy.

Pendennis, in contrast to all the other castles built under Henry VIII's orders, was built on top of the headland, perhaps in recognition of the weaknesses of St Mawes, which is overlooked by a hill and therefore vulnerable to attack by land. The form here was an artillery tower, with guns on two floors and on the roof. The castle's remoteness from the shoreline, however, had its drawbacks. Perhaps this was why a 'chemise' or circular gun platform was added, with a better command of the surrounding sea. A twin-towered gatehouse

was added on the landward side almost as an afterthought.

The Killigrews

Pendennis Headland was leased from a local landowner, John Killigrew, who had a house at Arwenack, to the north of the headland. Killigrew may have also supervised the construction of the castle. The Killigrews were from a family of Penryn merchants who aspired to upward mobility in the ranks of the Cornish gentry. Always keen to make a profit, however, they were also deeply involved in the activities of local shipowners and traders who often turned to piracy to make a living. This was to land them in trouble on more than one occasion.

The fear of invasion passed, but England was soon at war with France again, reviving worries about a French landing on the coast. The coastal fortifications were reviewed in 1545, and both castles (although not quite finished) were found to have sufficient cannon but 'a great lack of powder'.

On the accession of the Catholic Queen Mary in 1553, Thomas Treffry lost his job in a purge of Protestants. John Killigrew only held on to the captaincy of Pendennis by depositing £1,000 as a guarantee of his good behaviour.

ABOVE *John Killigrew, first captain of Pendennis, and his wife Elizabeth Trewinnard, from their memorial brass in Budock Church*

RIGHT *Looking from St Mawes towards Pendennis. You can see how Henry's castle is built on the crest of the hill*

NEW THREATS AND
NEW FORTIFICATIONS

In 1570, the political situation in Europe changed. Pope Pius V excommunicated Queen Elizabeth I and urged Catholic monarchs to invade England to depose her and restore the Catholic faith. England once again faced a threat from continental Europe, and in particular Spain, the strongest European power at that time.

The threat from Spain

John Killigrew died in 1567 and was succeeded by his son, another John, who was knighted. He too, however, sometimes found himself in conflict with the authorities and, like his father, spent some time in prison in London. The deputy governor of St Mawes, Justinian Talkarne, was also implicated in piracy and dismissed from his post. Hannibal Vyvyan, who had succeeded his father Michael as captain of St Mawes in 1561, proved entirely loyal to the Crown.

In 1574, a Spanish fleet gathered at Santander. A hurried survey of the castles found that repairs were needed. The gun platform at Pendennis was 'much decayed and almost unserviceable'. Emergency work was carried out, including new ditches and earthen banks around the headlands to protect the castles on their landward sides.

In the event, the Spanish fleet that sailed in 1578 was dispersed by gales, but the threat of invasion and raids remained. The great fleet of the Spanish Armada of 1588 passed the castles by, but a Spanish raiding party in 1593 burnt the Killigrews' own house at Arwenack, while in 1595 Spanish troops landed near Penzance, burning the town and nearby Newlyn and Mousehole.

Both Killigrew and Vyvyan repeatedly pressed for more guns, supplies and improved defences for both castles, but little was forthcoming.

The new fort at Pendennis

In 1595, the Lord Lieutenant of Cornwall, Sir Walter Ralegh, assessed the West Country's defences and warned that Pendennis could be a prime objective of any invasion force. From there, he claimed, they could control the whole of west Cornwall as a bridgehead and anchor 'the greatest fleet that ever swam'. In 1596, another huge Spanish fleet set sail, this time avoiding the English navy. Only sudden gales off Land's End which dispersed the ships prevented a landing. Afterwards it was discovered that the fleet was indeed heading for Pendennis, where the Spanish admiral Adelantado had planned to create an island by cutting the peninsula at its neck and using the headland as a bridgehead for invading England. Ralegh's muster of 500 men would have had to face an invasion force of 20,000!

This lucky escape prompted action. Ralegh and the Earl of Essex visited Pendennis and recommended that the defences should be improved. The militia, raised in October, were becoming restless since the invasion scare had passed, so Ralegh replaced them with two companies of regular soldiers.

Ralegh appointed Sir Nicholas Parker, a professional soldier who had served in Elizabeth's wars in support of the Protestant Dutch, to oversee the construction work. Paul Ivy was asked to plan and supervise the building of a 'trace' or ramparts on the headland around the Henrician castle. Parker may have known Ivy from his time in the Netherlands where Ivy had built fortifications. More recently Ivy had worked on defences in the Channel Islands, most importantly Elizabeth Castle on Jersey, which shares some similarities with Pendennis.

BELOW *Sir Walter Ralegh. Ralegh was Lord Lieutenant of Cornwall in the 1590s and deeply concerned with the defence of his native West Country against the Spanish threat*

At Pendennis, Ivy used ramparts and angle bastions to surround the high land of the peninsula. The low earthen ramparts provided the minimum target for attackers while providing maximum firepower for the defenders. Cannons mounted on the ramparts could command the area through 360° while the bastions allowed smaller guns to provide covering fire along the ramparts. The Lower Fort was an integral part of the design, acting as a powerful bastion nearer sea level. St Mawes may also have had angle bastions added to its lunettes at the same time.

Ivy estimated £1,000 for the job, but construction was soon in trouble. The 'exceeding hardness of the work, being of main rock', meant that changes had to be made and the costs rose. Ralegh was forced to beg for an extra £1,000 from the Queen and Privy Council.

The work was finally finished early in 1600 and Parker was appointed captain, as Pendennis may now have seemed too important to have a Killigrew in charge. John Killigrew, who had succeeded his father on the latter's death in 1584, had also inherited his father's links with local pirates and these dealings were now used as an excuse to imprison him in London.

Parker's requests for more guns and men were also granted, including guns taken from St Mawes, which he regarded as indefensible by land. Hannibal Vyvyan vigorously disputed this, but was eventually overruled by the Privy Council itself.

Peace with Spain came with the accession of James I in 1603. The newly constructed fort was now redundant and neglected. The garrison was downgraded, and often received pay years in arrears, forcing the men to eat limpets and pawn their bedding to buy food. The captaincy of Pendennis returned to the Killigrews in 1614. Sir Robert Killigrew constantly petitioned for money to improve the armament and state of the fort, but his requests were ignored.

ABOVE *From the air you can see clearly the shape of Paul Ivy's ramparts encompassing the high ground of Pendennis Headland*

THE CIVIL WAR AND
THE SIEGE OF PENDENNIS

The new defences of Pendennis and St Mawes were soon tested in action, not by enemy invaders but by fellow countrymen during the Civil War between King Charles I and Parliament in the 1640s.

Strengthening the land front

In 1627, the tense political situation with France and Spain once again prompted action. The military engineer Bernard Johnson was commissioned to repair the ramparts and reinforce the weak landward

LEFT *Charles, Prince of Wales, in 1642, aged 12, a detail from a portrait by William Dobson*

side of Pendennis' defences. He built a hornwork – an earthen rampart extending the defences to enclose the remaining high ground of the peninsula, with small semi-bastions and a ravelin (a forward detached gun position) to mount cannons. The effect would be to add further obstacles to any attacking force making a landward assault.

The loyalty of the Killigrews may have once again come into question, for in 1635 the captaincy was granted to Sir Nicholas Slanning, a professional soldier, MP for Penryn and a staunch supporter of King Charles I. Pendennis was equipped with 55 new pieces of ordnance.

King versus Parliament

At the start of the Civil War in August 1642, Pendennis and St Mawes were both held for the king. Falmouth was an important base for Royalists for the import of arms and essential supplies from the continent, paid for in part by Cornish tin. Privateers also operated from the harbour, attacking Parliamentary shipping to raise money for the war effort.

In 1643, Sir Nicholas Slanning joined Cornish troops marching north to fight the Parliamentarians, but was killed during the siege of Bristol. He was replaced as governor by Sir John Arundell of Trerice, already in his seventies, supported by his son Richard.

In 1644 the war reached Cornwall, as the Parliamentary army under the Earl of Essex advanced through Devon and Cornwall, until halted by their defeat at Lostwithiel. Charles's queen, Henrietta Maria, arrived at Pendennis in July 1644, fleeing ahead of Essex's army. She stayed at least one night at Pendennis before slipping away to safety in France on 14 July.

LEFT *A reconstruction by Ivan Lapper of how Pendennis may have looked during the siege. Note the Hornwork and the 'traverses', earthen banks running down from the castle to the sea to strengthen the land defences*

By late 1645 the tide of the war was turning against the Royalists, who were in retreat. The King's generals, Sir Ralph Hopton and Sir Edward Hyde, visited Pendennis to investigate how it could be strengthened to hold out as a bridgehead for foreign reinforcements. It was probably then that the advanced bastion and ramparts at Upton's Mount were started. If completed, they would have significantly strengthened the castle's landward defences. However, the work was never finished. Perhaps the soldiers employed on building them were needed elsewhere. One feature that was completed was a fort at Helford to defend the mouth of the Helford River and the convenient sheltered waters and landings beyond.

In early 1646 Prince Charles (the future Charles II) arrived, but on 2 March he too left Pendennis by sea, bound for the Isles of Scilly and then Jersey.

Hopton's defeated army surrendered at Truro five days later. The fortresses were excluded from this treaty, however, and Pendennis was reinforced with quality troops and stocked with cannon and supplies. The Royalist plan was to hold out in Pendennis until relief arrived from the continent.

The siege

The Parliamentarian general, Sir Thomas Fairfax, marched to the coast to attack the castles. On 12 March, St Mawes surrendered without a shot being fired. Its governor, Hannibal Bonythion, realised that the castle could not be defended against land attack. The fort at Helford followed soon after, reducing Royalist command of Falmouth Bay.

Pendennis held firm, however. There were about 1,000 men inside the fort, together with women and children. There was ammunition and food supplies for six weeks, and Sir John Arundell was defiant:

The castle was committed to my government by His Majesty ... [and] I resolve that I will here bury myself before I deliver up this castle to such as fight against His Majesty.

The Parliamentarians dug in for a long siege. They built a small fort for their cannon, flanked by deep ditches, effectively cutting off the peninsula. Parliamentary ships imposed a naval blockade. Both sides bombarded each other, with a beached warship left by Hopton, probably the *Great George,* using its cannon to strengthen significantly the castle's defences.

By early August morale in the Royalist camp was weakening. The king had already surrendered himself to the Scots, there was no sign of help from abroad, and there had been two unsuccessful attempts to buy surrender. Lack of food was causing dissent among the garrison. On 15 August Arundell agreed to terms for an 'honourable' surrender and on 17 August, after handing over all cannon and military stores, the garrison marched out

with flying colours, trumpets sounding, drums beating, matches lighted at both ends, bullets in the mouths, and every soldier 12 charges of powder ... all their own goods, bags and baggage with a safe convoy to Arwinck Downs.

Although accorded the full honours of war, the garrison was in a poor state. Over half were ill from malnutrition, and the remainder weak.

Pendennis and St Mawes were too valuable strategically to be dismantled, so the victorious commander of the siege, Colonel Richard Fortescue, was installed as governor with a garrison of 400.

NATIONAL PORTRAIT GALLERY

ABOVE *Sir Thomas Fairfax*

ABOVE TOP *A re-enactment group dressed as soldiers of the period. Pendennis Castle was the last but one stronghold holding out for the king in mainland England and Wales to surrender*

BELOW *Reconstruction by Ivan Lapper of the 'honourable' surrender*

NEGLECT AND RESTORATION

In 1660, Charles II returned from exile to be restored to the throne. One of his main backers in the West Country, who had acted as an envoy in the negotiations, was Sir Peter Killigrew, son of the captain of Pendennis before 1635. Killigrew was rewarded with the governorship of Pendennis and the grant of a charter for a new town – to be called 'Falmouth' – that the Killigrews had been developing next to their house at Arwenack. The new town grew steadily, especially as a base for ship repair and supply. In 1689, Falmouth became the principal port for Packet Boats – private ships officially hired to carry mail as well as passengers.

Gentle neglect

Wars with the Dutch and then the French left England's coast defences on a state of almost permanent alert. The most substantial change in the castles during this period was the building of the gatehouse and guard barracks at Pendennis. The latter are among the earliest purpose-built barracks in England, perhaps dating to the 1690s. Otherwise, the castles settled into a peaceful routine. Pendennis' garrison consisted of no more than a couple of gunners and a company (about 50 men) of 'invalids' –

retired or sick soldiers. These invalids lived with their families in cottages scattered about the fort and spent more time tending their gardens than on military duties.

Colonel Lilly's report

In 1715, Colonel Christian Lilly, the Board of Ordnance's engineer in charge of defences in the West Country, made a major survey of Pendennis and St Mawes. His report confirmed some of the neglect of the past seventy years:

> the earthworks of the body of the fort having been for many years neglected are now in a very ruinous condition ... the entrenchments of the outworks are in many places filled up and entirely covered with furze and bramble. ... [the gunners are] ignorant, inactive [and] drunken ... who should be replaced.

Lilly proposed clearing the redundant buildings within the ramparts, repairing the ramparts themselves and creating a new barrack block for 64 soldiers within the castle. He also proposed building a new storehouse. There are no records to confirm exactly when Lilly's recommendations at Pendennis and St Mawes were put into effect, but it appears that over the next thirty years most of his proposals were acted upon.

BELOW *Engraving by Samuel and Nathaniel Buck of St Mawes Castle, with Pendennis in the background, 1734. At this time the governorship of the castle usually went with the job of local MP, as up until the Great Reform Act of 1832 the small garrison had the right to elect their own MP*

The Elizabethan parapet of Pendennis was completely renewed, and a new nine-gun battery added to the south-east rampart. It also seems likely that the Long Platform and Crab Quay batteries outside the ramparts were reconstructed at the same time.

The castles still required regular maintenance. In the 1760s, part of the stone revetment of Carrick Mount Bastion collapsed, and in 1770 the Henrician castle was struck by lightning, dislodging 17 tons of stone and making it uninhabitable.

St Mawes during this period seems not to have undergone any major alterations, but the Sea Battery was armed with powerful cannon. This battery may have been created by Lilly after 1735 on the footings of the Tudor batteries flanking the blockhouse.

Invasion fears

During the eighteenth century Britain was involved in numerous wars that once again left the country in danger of invasion from continental Europe. The French made serious plans to invade in 1692, 1708, 1744-45, 1759 and 1762, but all failed due to poor weather, defeat or blockade by the British, or loss of surprise.

The best opportunity for success for Britain's enemies occurred in 1779, with France and Spain working together, and Britain preoccupied by the American War of Independence. On 16 August, a huge fleet was sighted off Land's End. Some 2,000 tin miners poured into Pendennis to reinforce it.

The Franco-Spanish objective had originally been the Isle of Wight or Portsmouth, or failing that, Plymouth, but poor co-ordination, sickness and lack of supplies forced a change of plan and Falmouth was selected as the bridgehead, as a preliminary to seizing the whole of Cornwall.

In the event, the indecision of the Spanish commander, Conde d'Orvilliers, caused the plan to fail and the invasion fleet retreated without attempting a landing. Once again the defences were reprieved.

Turner's romantic view of the castles, seen from St Mawes Harbour, c.1822

WAR AND PEACE

In 1789, revolution erupted in France. Britain was soon at war again, first against republican France and then against Napoleon. Once more, attention focused on Britain's coast defences. At Pendennis and St Mawes the renewed threat led to a new lease of life for the fortresses.

The French invasion threat

The French formulated fresh invasion plans, including a proposal to seize the West Country, although on the prompting of Irish nationalists the target was later made Ireland, with an attempted landing at Bantry Bay by a force of 15,000 men in 1796. In the early 1800s the invasion of England preoccupied Napoleon, who assembled a vast force across the Channel at Boulogne. The ramparts of Pendennis were repaired and a palisade and 'fraize' of stakes added. A new semi-circular battery was built below the rampart (Half Moon Battery) in 1793 and a similar battery built for four 24-pounder guns on St Anthony Head three years later.

The 'Key of Cornwall'

More changes were made in 1803-04 in response to a request to King George III from Lieutenant-General Simcoe:

Pendennis … secures the harbour at Falmouth, the Key of Cornwall, and which in the possession of an enemy might lead to the most disastrous consequences … the present and future situation of this country, in my most humble opinion, calls for the … occupation of Pendennis in the most judicious manner.

Raised 'cavaliers' were built on the bastions of Pendennis and additional magazines and stores built. Four wooden barrack huts were built on the parade ground and a substantial shed, much of which survives, was built for a field artillery train. A hospital was placed outside the ramparts where disease was less likely to infect the garrison. In 1804, both castles were described as being 'in a very respectable state of defence against an assault'.

The wars boosted Falmouth's role as a training centre and a depot for supplies, especially after 1808 as supply base to Wellington's army in Spain and Portugal, and as a centre for the packet ships. Lilly's storehouse of the 1730s was enlarged and a new brick and stone warehouse built between 1793 and 1811, which survives today.

Peace and neglect

With the arrival of peace with France in 1815 government spending on defence was cut dramatically and the castles were soon neglected. In 1817, the guns in the Grand Sea Battery at St Mawes were said to be on skids after their carriages had rotted away. The wooden barracks were sold or demolished, and those buildings which survived were left to decay, surrounded by gardens and vegetable plots. In the late 1820s the government even considered the complete demolition of Pendennis.

Henry VIII's castle at Pendennis, now

ABOVE *The storehouse built at Pendennis Castle during the Napoleonic wars*

RIGHT *Portrait of Lieutenant-Colonel Philip Melville, Governor of Pendennis Castle for most of the Napoleonic period. He was a survivor of the 'Black Hole of Calcutta' and the experience may have led to the extremes of emotion he is reported to have shown*

◁ THE MINERS MILITIA ▷

Defending the castles in an emergency in Tudor and Stuart times depended on calling up the militia, partly trained volunteers from the local area. The system allowed 100 men each to be 'mustered' to man Pendennis and St Mawes. Calling out the militia often led to complaints that the demands were excessive or unnecessary, especially when the supposed threat failed to materialise.

By the late eighteenth century, the militia and the handfuls of regular soldiers garrisoning forts like Pendennis were reinforced by local volunteers, who formed their own units. Army reforms in the mid-nineteenth century improved the training and quality of the militia. As the militia for Falmouth was mainly composed of men from the local Cornish tin mines, it became known as the Miners Militia. Its headquarters was moved from Truro to Pendennis.

In the early twentieth century, militia and volunteers were combined to create the Territorial Army we know today. The Miners Militia became the Duke of Cornwall's Royal Garrison Artillery.

The Pendennis Artillery Volunteers in 1800. The volunteers were a specialist militia artillery unit set up by Governor Melville during the Revolutionary and Napoleonic wars

known as Castle House, was the residence of the lieutenant-governor, the post itself by now a sinecure. In 1840, after the office of governor was finally abolished, it was leased out to a civilian, Francis Todd.

The invasion 'panics'

In the mid-1840s a wave of panic spread across the country caused by rumours of a planned French invasion. The new fears prompted a slow return to military order at Pendennis. The new Foreign Secretary, Lord Palmerston, was a strong advocate of coast defences. Government spending on fortifications was increased.

At Pendennis, emplacements for three 32-pounder guns were built on the southernmost sea-facing bastions in 1848 and a battery was half-constructed on Pendennis Point itself. Accommodation within the castle was overhauled and repaired, and the remaining soldiers' cottages cleared away.

The invasion scare evaporated after the overthrow of King Louis Philippe of France in 1848, but the rise to power of Louis Napoleon a few years later provoked more

unease. Pendennis was surveyed and it was discovered that most of the guns in the Half Moon and Crab Quay batteries were unserviceable.

By the end of 1854 three 32- and four 56-pounder guns on traversing platforms were in position in each bastion, and the Half Moon and Crab Quay batteries strengthened. At St Mawes, the Grand Sea Battery was completely rebuilt to mount four 10-inch and eight 8-inch shell guns. A new magazine was dug into the rear of the battery, flanked by special areas for mobile furnaces to heat cannon balls to make them 'red-hot' to be fired at the rigging of ships.

In 1859, the French launched an armoured steam frigate, *La Gloire,* to British consternation. Powered by steam or sail, it heralded the age of warships no longer constrained by wind and tide. Politicians and strategists claimed an invasion fleet could now reach British shores within hours, whatever the weather. Palmerston was now Prime Minister, and a comprehensive programme of fortifications was begun, although this time not including Falmouth.

NATIONAL PORTRAIT GALLERY

Lord Palmerston, a strong believer in the supposed military threat from France and the need for coast defences

NINETEENTH-CENTURY TRANSFORMATION

By the late nineteenth century, Falmouth's importance was no longer questioned. The port was used by the Navy as the first and last port of call for ships in the English Channel, and commands were sent to ships asking them to report to 'Falmouth for orders'. In 1868, the Falmouth Docks Company was formed. Although a private venture, its ship-repairing facility attracted the attention of the Navy and led to renewed interest in Falmouth's strategic significance.

A new threat

The focus of invasion fears was also moving away from the traditional enemy, France, towards a new threat, the newly unified Germany. By the late 1880s growing German military and naval power was causing concern. Germany had made it clear that it wished to create a powerful fleet that would allow it to trade and compete for overseas colonies. It could also be used to support a invasion.

Technological developments were rapidly changing the nature of warfare. Machine-guns meant that ramparts could be defended without the need for deep ditches or musketry galleries. Cordite explosive had replaced black gunpowder. Rifled guns firing pointed shells, breech-loading guns, steel barrels and quick-fire mechanisms all created changes in the range and efficiency of coast batteries. The invention of the depression range finder meant that targets could be measured more effectively. In the mid-1880s Falmouth became one of the first ports in the country to have an under-water 'electric minefield'. Observation posts were built from where the mines could be remotely detonated using electric current.

The coast fortress

In 1888, a report to the Defence Committee recommended that Falmouth's harbour should be better protected. In the early 1890s the recommendations were acted upon and Falmouth was designated a 'coast fortress'.

In the following years the defences of Falmouth were comprehensively upgraded. Three 6-inch breech-loading hydropneu-matic, or 'disappearing' guns were installed at Pendennis (see pages 10 and 12). An answering battery with two 6-inch guns on the other side of the channel was set up at St Anthony Head, in preference to St Mawes. In addition, batteries were created in Pendennis' East Bastion and in the field above St Mawes Castle, each for two 12-pounder quick-fire guns, while in the channel between the two castles was the 'electric minefield'.

The strategy behind these defences was that the big guns would be used to counter any naval bombardment by enemy ships offshore. The quick-fire guns and minefield, by contrast, could counter any attacks by enemy torpedo boats on battleships at anchor in the harbour or attempts to sink a vessel and block the harbour entrance. Electric searchlights allowed the defences to operate effectively by night as well as by day.

Reconstruction drawing by Ivan Lapper of the 6-inch 'disappearing gun' in One Gun Battery as it may have appeared in about 1900

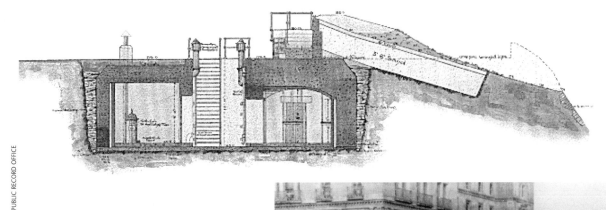

A regular garrison

This modernization of Falmouth's defences between 1894 and 1904 reasserted the port's significance and gave it the distinction of being the only mercantile harbour on the south coast to be made a 'defended port'. As a mark of their new importance, the batteries were given a garrison of regular soldiers, the 105th Regiment of Royal Garrison Artillery, and a new barracks at Pendennis, with service buildings, such as a cookhouse and bath house, built to accommodate them. Provision was also made for the gunners at St Anthony. In front of the Henrician castle a headquarters building for the Miners Militia was built in an extravagant mock-Tudor style.

Both regular and militia troops held practice exercises to train with the guns. In May 1903 the defences were put to the test by a surprise 'attack' by the Royal Navy's Torpedo Boat Flotilla from Devonport. Whether by design, or whether the manoeuvres revealed a weakness, additional 12-pounder batteries were subsequently built at Pendennis and St Mawes.

The co-ordination of the defences was disrupted, however, by rivalries between the Army and Navy over the division of responsibility for the mines and coastal batteries, and in 1906 the 6-pounders at Crab Quay were removed. In 1909, dissatisfaction with the hydropneumatic guns seems have led to the decision to remodel the Half Moon Battery to mount more conventional 6-inch guns. These now became the harbour's main defence. The 105th Regiment was withdrawn in 1911 and responsibility for the guns now fell to the newly created Territorial Army regiment formed from the Miners Militia.

ABOVE TOP *Cross-section through the quick-fire gun battery in East Bastion from the original plans, 1901*

ABOVE *Soldiers of the 105th Regiment of Royal Garrison Artillery parading in front of the Falmouth Hotel, early 1900s*

–• ELECTRIC MINEFIELD •–

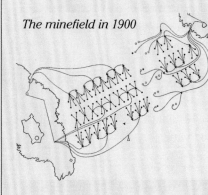

The minefield in 1900

From the mid-1880s onwards, Falmouth Harbour was protected by one of the first electric minefields in the world. The minefield was specifically designed to combat torpedo boats operating at night. A network of explosive mines was seeded across the mouth of the estuary.

Aided by electric searchlights, observers would track an enemy vessel by telescope. As the telescope moved, it would pass over brass studs on a large table, completing an electric circuit by underwater cable to detonate the explosive mine closest to the enemy vessel.

THE CASTLES IN THE TWENTIETH CENTURY

ABOVE *Mata Hari, the dancer and alleged German spy, who was detained on a liner docking at Falmouth in 1917. She was sent to France where she was eventually tried and executed for spying*

RIGHT *Soldiers and sailors in a tented canteen set up on Hornwork Common during the First World War*

Far from losing importance in the twentieth century, the castles in wartime became the command centre of the defences for the whole of south-west Cornwall, stretching from Land's End to St Austell, covering the Western Approaches and the vital entrance to the English Channel. They thus continued to fulfil the role they had been built for 400 years earlier.

The First World War

The outbreak of war in August 1914 was greeted by popular enthusiasm. In Falmouth, the gun crews had fired across the bows of three non-enemy vessels caught disobeying the wartime harbour regulations in the space of less than a week. Military planners, however, knew that despite naval superiority British mastery of the seas was not assured. The threat showed itself as real that December when four German cruisers bombarded the towns of Whitby, Hartlepool and Scarborough on the north-east coast of England.

All Britain's ports were defended against attack. Trenches and barbed wire were created to add extra lines of defence. Falmouth itself became a training camp and port of departure for new recruits before they joined colleagues in the trenches in France.

Although the feared German invasion never occurred, the progress of the war did reveal new threats against which the coast batteries were much less prepared. One was the use of submarines (U-boats). Convoys sought the safety of Falmouth Haven, and U-boats were sunk by decoy ships at the mouth of the estuary on more than one occasion. A huge submarine boom of iron hoops was strung between St Anthony and the Helford River. Friendly shipping passed through a 'gate' in the boom supervised by a permanently moored fishing boat.

Another new threat was that of bombardment from the air from Zeppelin airships. A network of observers was set up, a night-time blackout imposed and primitive anti-aircraft guns installed.

The war ended on 11 November 1918. The army was cut in size and the defences downgraded. The guns were maintained at the Half Moon Battery for occasional practice, but those at St Anthony were dismantled in 1924. The Henrician castles were scheduled as Ancient Monuments and opened to the public.

Between the wars

In the inter-war years, the military threat from airpower increased dramatically. There were genuine fears about the use of aerial bombing and gas attacks. Falmouth was only a category 'B', or second-ranking port in defence plans in the 1930s, chosen for the storage of fuel: storage tanks encased in concrete were built at the dock end of the Pendennis Headland. The guns of the Half Moon Battery were removed in July 1938, but the growing threat of war meant that a few months later Falmouth was upgraded to a category 'A' port.

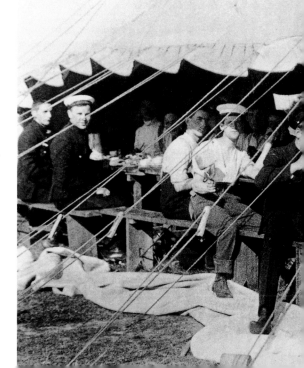

The Second World War

When war was declared on 3 September 1939, Falmouth had no major coast defence guns. Defence plans were soon put into operation, however, to create a fully defended port – Fixed Defences Falmouth. St Anthony was re-armed with Mk VII 6-inch guns twelve days later, and within the month building work had started on new emplacements at Half Moon Battery. The two 6-inch guns there were ready for action by November 1939, manned by Cornwall Heavy Regiment 193 Heavy Battery. New searchlights and telecommunications equipment were installed. Nissen huts were built within Pendennis Castle and on Hornwork Common to accommodate an ever-changing succession of soldiers. The Henrician castle at Pendennis became the headquarters of the Commander Fixed Defences Falmouth and the officers' mess. Once again, the harbour was protected by submarine booms and a system designed to 'examine' all shipping entering or leaving the harbour.

After the fall of France in 1940, Falmouth became part of the front line of defence. An air raid on Falmouth in July 1940 in which over 40 people were killed highlighted the need for defences from air attack. Anti-aircraft guns were installed. In December, concrete anti-strafing canopies were built over the 6-inch gun emplacements and permanent barrage balloons tethered above. St Mawes also had a barrage balloon station. New battery observation posts were constructed for the guns where the Battery Commander could receive information and control the guns and searchlights.

In mid-1941 new twin 6-pounder quick-fire gun batteries were installed, one at St Mawes, in the field to the north of the castle, one at Middle Point and a 12-pounder battery placed on the apron of One Gun Battery.

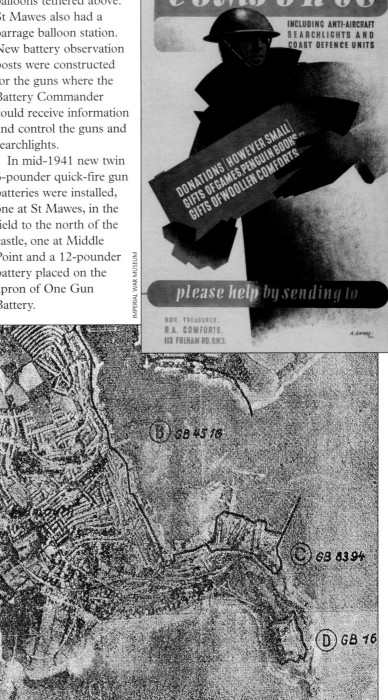

ABOVE TOP *A poster from the Second World War appealing for gifts and 'comforts' for those manning the coast batteries*

ABOVE *A German aerial reconnaisance photograph, with the harbour, docks and Pendennis Castle highlighted*

FALMOUTH AT WAR

· TOTAL WAR ·

Rapid changes in the technology and nature of warfare in the twentieth century encouraged new ways to defend the coast from attack and invasion. War now became 'total war', involving the whole community, and attack could come from land, sea and air. Improvements were made in the design, range, and targeting of guns. Radar, range finders and electronic transmission (magslip) improved observation, target information and command procedures. Anti-aircraft guns were introduced to counter the threat from aerial attack. Fixed guns needed concrete gun-houses or anti-strafing canopies to protect them during a *blitzkrieg* attack when enemy dive-bombers would try to destroy such fixed defences.

29 February 1944

At 0058 hours Fire Commander informed that the Navy had identified plot as hostile and allocated No. E11F.

Alarm was sounded and all batteries in Fire Command put at immediate readiness. Target was now at 12,600 yards and was coming rapidly at 35 knots.

At 0120 hours target stationery at 6,150 yards, and the first salvo was fired. Immediately target began to move away from battery rapidly, increasing speed to 35 knots,

At 0126 hours, immediately after radar had reported round as range, flash was seen on water which lasted for 15 seconds and was followed by a whitish cloud of smoke.

At 0127 searchlights were exposed for three minutes but no targets were picked up.

At 0132 hours battery again opened fire. Target was now at 13,800 yards and rapidly increasing to 18,000 yards. Radar set continued to follow target until well out of range. Echo split into three distinct echoes, indicating at least three vessels.

LEFT *Wartime photograph of the Battery Observation Post in use*

BELOW *A 6-inch gun firing at night, 1942*

ABOVE *An extract from the log book for Half Moon Battery*

The Falmouth coast defences first saw enemy action on 26 February 1943 when Half Moon Battery fired at a target, probably a German E-boat, which was forced to alter course and make for the French coast. The last occasion the guns fired at an enemy target was in March 1944 when E-boats were detected by radar at extreme range.

This action occurred during the build-up to the invasion of France – D-Day – on 6 June 1944. Falmouth itself was a scene of busy preparations, as many of the troops bound for the Normandy beaches left from the port. Falmouth had already become an important port of call for the North Atlantic convoys and a disembarkation point for arriving US troops, so much so that Falmouth was locally known as the '49th state of the Union'.

The threat from the air

The docks at Falmouth were a regular target for German air raids. The Germans had good photographs of the town and its defences: visits by a German warship, the *Schleswig-Holstein*, before the war had obviously reaped results. Tucked in behind Pendennis Headland, the docks were a difficult target to hit, and bombs often fell in the sea or on surrounding areas. There were several raids in July 1940, including one on 10 July that sunk several ships in the harbour. In March 1941, a parachute mine wrecked part of St Anthony Fort.

The worst raid on Falmouth was on 30 May 1944, just before D-Day. There was extensive damage along the sea front and numerous casualties. But the most serious damage was caused when a secret fuel depot at Swanpool was hit, and firefighters had to struggle for days to contain a river of burning petrol from flowing downhill towards the houses of Swanvale village.

RIGHT *Painting by John Platt of a convoy arriving off St Anthony Head Lighthouse (1942). During the 'Battle of the Atlantic', Falmouth Harbour was often the first port of call and safe harbour for numerous convoys of merchant ships and their naval escorts, after the dangerous journey across the ocean*

Secret war

The coast and creeks of Cornwall were ideal for secret warfare activity. Both the Fal and Helford estuaries were used by the Special Intelligence Service (SIS) and the Special Operations Executive (SOE) as bases for activities in Brittany, mingling with the French fishing fleets, transporting agents, rescuing escaped prisoners-of-war and supplying the French Resistance.

In March 1942, Falmouth was the base for the flotilla of small ships that transported the commandos for the raid on the dry docks at St Nazaire. Great secrecy also surrounded the build-up to D-Day. The Fal, and its neighbouring estuaries, were used to load landing craft and supply boats, and sections of the prefabricated 'Mulberry Harbour', before the Channel crossing to the Normandy coast.

ABOVE *A Bofors light anti-aircraft gun. Several of these were positioned around Pendennis Castle to protect the gun batteries against aerial attack*

NATIONAL MARITIME MUSEUM

CONSERVATION IN THE FUTURE

Throughout the late 1940s and early 1950s the batteries around Falmouth Haven continued to be maintained and used for practice by various Territorial Army units. However, the new threat posed by nuclear warfare rendered traditional coast defences redundant. In 1956 the Coast Artillery Branch of the Army was disbanded and the equipment cut up for scrap. The castles returned to the guardianship of the Ministry of Works, which was succeeded by English Heritage in 1984.

The historical importance of Henry VIII's castles was recognised early on in this century, and work was done to conserve and record the structures. However, it is only in recent years that there been a stronger awareness of the importance of the Pendennis Headland defences as a whole and the wider importance of the complete system of coast defences around Falmouth Haven. Studies and research have revealed the extent, variety and importance of these defences. The people of Falmouth, too, have come forward to share their memories of the castles in the twentieth century. This has all added to our understanding of the defences.

In 1995 there was a successful bid for money from the Heritage Lottery Fund from English Heritage, the National Trust, Cornwall County Council and Carrick District Council.

At Pendennis this has contributed to improvements to the environment of the area, allowing new sections of the defences such as the Half Moon Battery to be opened up to visitors. The Hornwork Common has been grassed over and the former car parks relocated. At St Anthony Head parts of the fort have been rediscovered and made accessible.

This process will continue into the future in order to safeguard the important elements of these coast defences.

RIGHT *The Henrician castle at Pendennis under floodlights*

Further reading

Colvin, H. M. (ed.) *The History of the King's Works*, 2 vols, 1963.
Longmate, N. *Island Fortress: The defence of Great Britain* 1603–1945, 1991.
Pasfield Oliver, S. *Pendennis and St Mawes*, 1875 (facsimile edition published 1984).
Saunders, A. *Fortress Britain: Artillery fortification in the British Isles and Ireland*, 1989.